Cryptocurrency

A Comprehensive Manual On Constructing Mining Rigs
And Engaging In The Mining Of Bitcoin, Ethereum, And
Various Other Cryptocurrencies

*(How To Utilize The Four Pillars Of Cryptocurrency
Investing To Generate Automatic Wealth)*

Quintin Daniel

TABLE OF CONTENT

Introduction 1

Gaining Insight Into The Prevalent Cryptocurrencies 4

Trading In Cryptocurrency 31

Blocks And Transactions 50

Miscellaneous Matters And Concerns 69

The Inherent Shortcomings Of Decentralised Finance 91

Optimizing The Well-Being Of The Body And Mind 101

Rsi Trading Strategy 107

The Contemporary Realm Of Blockchain 121

Introduction

What is cryptocurrency? Fundamentally speaking, cryptocurrency functions as a digital or virtual form of currency that employs cryptographic techniques to ensure security and operates in a decentralized manner, thereby eluding control from centralized entities, such as governmental bodies or financial institutions. Cryptocurrency is dependent upon a decentralized ledger technology referred to as a blockchain, which facilitates the secure and transparent recording and verification of transactions.

In recent years, there has been considerable discourse surrounding the notion of cryptocurrency, notably highlighted by the widely recognized instance of Bitcoin. Nevertheless, there exists a plethora of numerous cryptocurrencies, each possessing its distinct attributes and applications. This literary work will delve into the chronicles and progression of cryptocurrency, encompassing the genesis of Bitcoin and its pivotal position as the inaugural decentralized digital currency. We will additionally explore the fundamental technical aspects of cryptocurrency, scrutinize the underlying economic principles governing it, and analyze the diverse practical applications to which it can be utilized.

Furthermore, we will appraise the legal and regulatory framework surrounding cryptocurrency, while also analyzing its ongoing social and cultural ramifications. Furthermore, we will take into account the potential hazards and obstacles confronting the cryptocurrency sector, alongside the promising prospects it holds for its forthcoming trajectory. In conclusion, we will offer valuable guidance for individuals who are keen on utilizing or allocating funds in cryptocurrency.

In the subsequent chapter, we will examine the historical roots of cryptocurrency, along with the evolution of electronic cash and digital currency preceding the emergence of Bitcoin. Remain engaged to acquire further knowledge about the early trailblazers who established the foundations for the decentralized digital revolution.

Gaining Insight Into The Prevalent Cryptocurrencies

Bitcoin was the inaugural form of digital currency. It was the inaugural cryptocurrency to garner extensive fascination and draw the attention of the digital sphere and the traditional currency realm, along with regulators and governmental entities alike. The emergence of BTC can be attributed to the blockchain system, which ultimately served as the prototype for subsequent blockchains and ledgers. Despite the implementation of other forks and iterations, BTC and its blockchain persist as the fundamental centerpiece of the cryptocurrency realm. In the realm of cryptocurrencies, two overarching domains can be observed. The initial category encompasses the BTC domain, while the subsequent class pertains to the altcoins realm.

The realm of alternative cryptocurrencies consists of renowned digital currencies such as Bitcoin, Ethereum, Ripple, Dogecoin, and also encompasses several lesser-known, more recent forms of digital currency. The initial matter that would inevitably arise in the mind of a discerning reader is the rationale behind the proliferation of various cryptocurrencies, the processes leading to their emergence, and the impact they have on trading dynamics.

Bitcoin

Due to the absence of a central governing body or sovereign backing, as well as the absence of substantial server maintenance or exorbitant initial expenses, there are minimal obstacles for individuals interested in establishing their own cryptocurrency.

Fundamentally, you have the option to establish your own form of currency at present and become part of the extensive realm of alternative digital currencies, comprising over one thousand distinct cryptocurrencies. Indeed, the current circulation of cryptocurrencies surpasses one thousand, representing an exponential increase of tenfold in comparison to the collective number of sovereign currencies across the globe. In aggregate, they represent an estimated value of around $200 million. Although this may appear insignificant, particularly when juxtaposed with the global dollar-trading volume of approximately five trillion dollars, it is imperative to factor in an additional metric when engaging in such comparisons. The dollar serves as the fundamental and primary currency of the global economy, serving as the means of exchange for over 90% of all international trade transactions. Indeed, the proportion exceeds 90%, albeit not reaching the entirety of 100%, due to the waning predominance of the USD on the global stage and the emergence of nations such as China engaging in international commerce utilizing the yuan. The dollar has a notably lengthier history. Bitcoin is significantly younger when juxtaposed with the dollar and operates in a fundamentally distinct manner.

There exist two perspectives from which one can approach the concept of Bitcoin. One approach is to examine it based on its currency composition. This constitutes the component that is eligible for acquisition, sale, possession, exchange, or utilization in the capacity of a medium of exchange for the procurement of commodities and services. The opposing aspect to consider is the implementation of trust standardization. Due to the utilization of blockchain technology, Bitcoin possesses the capability to authenticate and substantiate not solely transactions, but also purchases. Therefore, it possesses practical applicability in real-life contexts. Once a transaction is executed and recorded in the blockchain, the inherent replication across the entire system ensures its permanent status and complete visibility. The utilization of advanced features inherent in Bitcoin has rendered it increasingly enticing for various reasons. Despite the prohibition of BTC in certain nations worldwide, the magnitude of its emergence remains a crucial factor that cannot be disregarded or understated.

Bitcoin possesses inherent brand value, coupled with the superiority of its algorithm and accompanying applications in comparison to recent market entrants. The intrinsic value of Bitcoin lies in its resistance to fraudulent activities and its inability to modify past transactions. It eliminates the factor of trust and provides a formalized process for the transaction while ensuring privacy remains intact. Furthermore, Bitcoin possesses a distinct advantage over other currencies due to its consistent and well-documented track record of success. The aforementioned characteristic is reflected in the pricing mechanism of Bitcoin across two dimensions.

The initial point to consider is that its price is notably higher compared to the other coins. Additionally, it exhibits greater price volatility compared to alternative cryptocurrencies. For traders, this implies that there are two benefits that can be obtained from this situation. The initial point to consider is that your investment gains enhanced security in terms of liquidity, and secondly, this signifies an increase in trading prospects within a given day. Consequently, the concept of swing trading or day trading is swiftly emerging as a viable means of generating wealth.

"Please take note of the following essential information regarding Bitcoin, which will be beneficial for your trading approach:

Most extensive developer community

First-mover advantage

Highest liquidity

Largest user base

Proven security

Store of value

Far more accessible

These factors provide considerable incentive for incorporating BTC as the cornerstone of your trading strategy, albeit not obligatory. However, it is imperative that you grasp the intricacies of BTC and the subsequent advancements, as its acceptance, progression, and backing will depend on the stability of the global market. BTC has emerged as the principal indicator of the cryptocurrency market and industry.

Altcoins

Alternative cryptocurrencies present a robust and persuasive narrative in their own right. Although BTC holds the foremost position in the field, the cryptocurrency industry would not have flourished to this extent if it solely relied on one player. Currently, there exists in excess of one thousand alternative cryptocurrencies in circulation within the market. The most substantial among these is Ethereum (subject to potential modifications at the time of release or shortly thereafter). Furthermore, there exist lesser-known alternative cryptocurrencies, commonly referred to as altcoins, which are within the reach of any aspiring entrepreneur seeking to develop a proprietary blockchain.

One has the ability to devise their own alternative cryptocurrency and designate it with any desired name. You are not required to obtain authorization or a license, and it can serve as a medium of exchange for any transaction. One could potentially establish a pizzeria establishment wherein XCoin, a specified digital currency, is exclusively utilized as the accepted form of payment. Additionally, the proprietor could offer the opportunity to purchase XCoin alongside the pizza, providing customers with a means to obtain this digital currency. Ultimately, the coin serves as a mere symbol denoting both the intention to engage in transactions and the assigned value for the exchange.

With the utilization of those same concepts, a plethora of altcoins have been introduced to the market, each presenting distinct ideas that are predicated upon the same foundational framework. This has constituted a significant advancement, and rather than detracting from BTC, it has bolstered the overall market, thereby resulting in an increase in BTC valuation. What is the advantage or utility you derive from that? It presents you with a unique chance to engage in market participation, capitalizing on the dynamics, value appreciation, development, and progression of every participant entering the market.

One must establish an equilibrium between the newly introduced coin and the one that has been present in the market for a considerable duration. It is imperative that you identify the option that instills a feeling of security and reliability prior to engaging in any transaction. Hence, when engaging in trading activities, it is advisable to restrict oneself to a single coin or a limited number of coins, rather than focusing solely on a specific coin. Generally, you would aspire to acquire expertise in, for example, the comparison between BTC and Ethereum. Or, BTC vs Monero. The specific pairing carries no significance, however, it is imperative for you to maintain a comprehensive understanding of the coins, encompassing a minimum of two pairs. Even if you engage in day trading, it is crucial to possess a fundamental understanding of the specific currency in which you specialize. This knowledge will enable you to make prompt and astute decisions, enhancing your ability to identify and seize lucrative opportunities as they emerge.

After obtaining a preliminary understanding of the pairing in which you aspire to attain expertise, it is important to acquire the necessary knowledge to elevate your proficiency. Additionally, it is advisable to undertake the study of at least two additional pairings, resulting in a total of four pairs. BTC is included as a constituent in two of the aforementioned pairs, yet it is absent in the remaining two pairs. Suppose we consider the comparison between BTC and Ethereum, and BTC and Litecoin. A potential alternative for the third comparison could involve examining the dynamics between Ethereum and both Bitcoin and Ripple. These options are not intended to provide guidance on the specific pairs you should prioritize; rather, they serve as exemplifications of the breadth of knowledge your repertoire should encompass. Among these four currency pairs, it is only necessary to monitor four distinct currencies. This will facilitate comprehension of the dynamics between individual entities. Additionally, it is a highly effective means of acquiring a comprehensive understanding of your field of expertise. Having worked as a trader in the past, my primary areas of focus were the currency pairs involving the US Dollar, Great British Pound, and Japanese Yen.

This presented a broader range of prospects in cross trading and arbitrage.

Despite the fact that the cryptocurrency market lacks the liquidity and swiftness of the currency market, it will ultimately reach that level; therefore, your efforts invested in practicing with it will yield favorable outcomes in the long run. In addition to the aforementioned long-term advantage, the capacity to concentrate solely on a limited number of currencies and avail oneself of a broader range of cross-trading opportunities allows for an enhanced return on investment.

Despite my preemptively discussing strategies that are presented later in the book, allow me to provide an illustrative example to elucidate the advantages of concentration on three or four currencies and engaging in cross trading between them.

There may be occasions where an advantageous trading opportunity of sufficient value and risk does not present itself within a single counter. In such instances, it would be prudent to divert your attention to alternative options. In the event that BTC experiences a decline in activity, one should not expect to encounter significant prospects in the BTC market as compared to Ethereum or Litecoin. However, it is possible to observe some level of activity occurring between Litecoin and Ripple. Consequently, possessing a versatile skill set in these respective markets would offer the opportunity to capitalize on such fluctuations. In the realm of day trading and swing trading, the level of prosperity one attains is intricately linked to the quantity of high-caliber trades executed, the ratio of successful outcomes to failures, and the frequency of market entries and exits. When one obtains further opportunities to penetrate the market by comprehending the characteristics of additional currency pairs, their interplay and relative valuation, they shall discover additional prospects for executing trades with commensurate rewards.

Presented before you are ten of the foremost alternative coins currently available in the market. Please be advised that the options available for trade far exceed a thousand in number. Nonetheless, the following list comprises merely ten select options that you might find desirable. The remaining options are not currently suitable as trading opportunities and will not become so unless they possess a compelling rationale for generating profit potential.

Ethereum

Ripple

Litecoin

Dash

NEM

Ethereum Classic

Monero

Zcash

Decred

PIVX

Marketability encompasses more than simply the cost factor. An item may possess great intrinsic worth, but devoid of any volatility, it offers no prospects for trading. If the market exhibits excessive volatility, it imparts diminished levels of security for trading. There must be a harmonious equilibrium between the degree of market volatility and the level of market liquidity. The optimal method for conducting coin trades is to ensure the presence of ample liquidity coupled with significant levels of volatility.

Why? Due to the absence of sufficient liquidity, volatility may arise. During this particular event, if you were to engage in market entry and trade the cryptocurrency, you may encounter difficulties when attempting to exit. Furthermore, the aforementioned trade has the potential to generate a temporary positive return, only to eventually result in a negative outcome due to the delay in locating a suitable counterparty to finalize the transaction. When considering liquidity, it can be observed that a market becomes more liquid as it gains popularity and amasses a larger user base. This increased liquidity in turn reduces the likelihood of the currency experiencing volatile price swings as a result of temporary buying and selling activities. This factor contributes to Bitcoin's higher valuation compared to other alternative cryptocurrencies, as it offers superior liquidity. The liquidity premium incorporates the impact of instantaneous entry and exit, thereby ensuring that the price displayed on your trading interface closely aligns with the actual execution price of a trade.

Liquidity

There is undoubtedly a fervent desire to develop the succeeding cryptocurrency to the likes of bitcoin, or even exceed its prominence. Numerous investments amounting to millions, and in some cases, even hundreds of millions, have been made by traditional currency investors with the aim of establishing their dominance in the realm of cryptocurrency for the foreseeable future. Consequently, what transpires is the manifestation of virtual representations comprised of fragments of digital information, which possess the potential to amass monetary worth exceeding $5000, similar to the case of Monero shortly after its inception. Each cryptocurrency possesses a distinct risk profile, which is determined by its level of liquidity.

The overall value, price, strength, and confidence that fans and followers place in a specific asset are primarily influenced by the asset's liquidity. Consider gold as an illustrative case. It primarily consists of metallic properties that elicit curiosity, yet ultimately it remains an ordinary constituent within the periodic table. It is the inherent fascination that humans attribute to it which confers value upon it. The aforementioned statement also applies to the valuation of digital currencies. It is the intrinsic worth ascribed to it by human conduct. As individuals increase their purchasing of it, there is a corresponding rise in their trading of it—leading to a gradual transformation of it into the universally accepted medium of exchange. Similar to how the USD gained global prominence. But everything starts somewhere.

In order to excel in the realm of cryptocurrency, one must acquire comprehensive knowledge of its considerable popularity and thoroughly assimilate numerous pivotal factors through diligent examination. The most skilled traders possess a innate comprehension of the mechanics of currencies and their reactions to market events.

What is the process for selecting currencies for trading? Regardless of whether it involves solely cryptocurrency exchanges or transactions between fiat and cryptocurrency, you must ascertain the currency pairing that offers the highest profitability. That is the feature that enables you to efficiently execute the transactions. Working with volatile coins can be advantageous as long as you can procure the required liquidity to enter and exit the market. Liquidity holds utmost significance.

However, concerns arise in relation to the level of liquidity exhibited by recently established coins. Please compare Bitcoin against Monero. The value of BTC continues to surpass that of inexperienced individuals, yet it remains conducive to implementing a trading strategy. In this particular scenario, what we observe is the presence of BTC as the foundational asset, with certain portions thereof being utilized for the acquisition of Monero. In this manner, you can derive advantages from the established coin's stability, while also capitalizing on the possible growth of the nascent coin. This strategy is robust and it is recommended that you incorporate it into your trading activities.

In accordance with convention, it would generally take the following form:

Initiate the process of creating an account by providing a designated quantity of BTC. In this instance, allow me to present an illustration using 100 BTC as a demonstrative scenario, while considering your initial possession of 200 BTC (recollecting the principle of allocating 50%). Subsequently, employ the BTC to allocate among a few trading methodologies. The initial option entails utilizing BTC to procure the designated currency of your choice, for instance, Monero. The initial tranche of acquisition would constitute approximately 10% of the overall investment valuation. This constitutes your overarching strategic approach. You buy this as a value investor. Subsequently, you allocate approximately 15% of your Bitcoin holdings towards Monero, employing a price point that reflects a swing trading strategy, premised on short-term investment over a period of few days.

Ultimately, a quarter of your available capital is allocated towards the acquisition of Monero, specifically for the purpose of engaging in daily trading activities.

This represents a viable approach that can be utilized. If you have a positive outlook on Monero, then you would implement this particular strategy. If you hold a pessimistic view of Monero, it is advisable to engage in direct short selling of the coin using your dollar-denominated account. It is important to note that each coin will exhibit distinct movements compared to its counterpart due to variations in their relative strength.

Allow me to elucidate my intended meaning.

Consider the possibility of forecasting a long-term appreciation of Monero, and subsequently implementing the aforementioned strategy. In this manner, you are generating profits through the long-term appreciation, short-term appreciation, and short-term retracement, respectively. Additionally, you are profiting from the daily fluctuations that occur. One might potentially find themselves holding a long position in Monero and a short position in Monero across various timeframes, thereby generating profits from both simultaneously. That represents the optimal scenario and is the desired course of action in implementing the trading strategies.

A significant number of my clients frequently inquire as to why they should engage in the sale of a coin when they hold a positive long-term sentiment. The response is that one should seek to capitalize on the marginal fluctuations that occur during an upward or downward movement. There exist a multitude of prospects within any given trade, and it is imperative to optimize your entry and exit points in order to attain a heightened return on your equivalent investment.

This practice is commonly referred to as "market scalping," and it presents a lucrative opportunity for financial gain, particularly if you familiarize yourself with the specific characteristics of the currency in which you specialize. This elucidates the significance of liquidity. If one finds themselves operating within a fluid market, it is possible to leverage the liquidity for the purpose of generating profits. One can capitalize on both upward and downward fluctuations in order to profit from extended periods of value growth.

However, as a trader, one cannot solely rely on the fundamentals in order to execute a trade. Dependence on foundational principles constitutes merely a quarter of your overall trading strategy. The remaining 75% encompasses a strategy grounded in statistical analysis and historical patterns.

Volatility

Concurrently with the presence of volatility, one must also consider the element of liquidity. This metric presents a more challenging assessment of a currency's suitability for investment. A fluctuating currency is influenced by a variety of factors. Certain currencies possess inherent volatility due to various attributes that underlie them. Subsequently, there exist assets characterized by volatility arising from their limited ownership and transaction activity. Consequently, whenever a potential buyer emerges, they trigger a sell order, thereby transforming the market into a buyer's domain.

In a buyer's market, the purchaser can afford to be patient and wait until the seller reduces their asking price due to the urgency of liquidating their asset. Alternatively, the opposite scenario may also be plausible. Upon the buyer's arrival at the market, should they desire to make a purchase, it becomes necessary for them to increase the price beyond that which was last traded. This increment is intended to allure the seller into participating in the market and relinquishing their portion. This gives rise to an ersatz pricing situation, wherein it effectively represents the additional compensation demanded by the seller to deviate from their original intentions of not selling, or the buyer to deviate from their original intentions of not purchasing. As the market becomes less liquid, the disparity in prices between buyers and sellers becomes increasingly wider. As market conditions become less voluminous, subsequent trades are expected to differ significantly from their preceding counterparts. With a limited market, it assumes the character of an individual vendor or purchaser, relinquishing any semblance of predictability. And thus, there is a distortion in the pricing.

When making a selection of a currency, it is imperative—as consistently emphasized throughout this literature—to ascertain that the chosen currency possesses a commendable degree of market liquidity, thereby mitigating the severity of its volatility. Liquidity serves a dual purpose, encompassing not only the ability to execute trades promptly but also gain a comprehensive understanding of the price data appearing on the displayed interface. The fact that volatile markets are influenced by low trading volumes has a tendency to disrupt automated trading systems and indicators used for identifying optimal buying and selling points. The fundamental principle underlying these metrics is the availability of buyers and sellers at all times, ensuring that pricing remains as dynamic as practicable.

Avoid engaging with illiquid markets unless you are committed to pursuing long-term gains derived from executing strategic currency initiatives. If you possess the inclination and capability to retain or relinquish your entire investment, it presents a prudent strategy, provided that you have aligned it with the appropriate objective. However, should you solely possess the intent of being a trader seeking financial gains, it would be advisable to refrain from engaging in illiquid markets.

Trading In Cryptocurrency

What is cryptocurrency trading? Similar to conventional stock market trading, cryptocurrency trading entails the act of engaging in short-term purchasing and selling of digital currencies. Arguably the most renowned 'transaction' in perpetuity is the Hanyecz pizza exchange in 2010, entailing the barter of 10,000 bitcoins for a pair of pizzas, with each pizza commanding a value exceeding $80,000,000 at the moment this instructional manual was authored.

Drawing a comparison between trading and investing; investing entails the deliberate acquisition of cryptocurrency followed by its prolonged retention. The objective of this endeavor is for the currency to appreciate in value during the specified time period. It necessitates the investor to endure periods of market decline, while anticipating that the asset's value will subsequently rebound and ultimately surpass its initial loss.

On the contrary, trading involves analyzing the comparatively brief tenure of holding a cryptocurrency with the objective of attaining expedited (and typically modest) financial gains. In order to accomplish this, it is imperative to make purchases during periods of price depreciation and subsequently sell once the value has appreciated and attained the target profit threshold. In general, endeavoring to mitigate ownership during periods of decline.

There exist a multitude of trading methodologies, including Position Trading, Swing Trading, Day Trading, and Scalp Trading. These trading styles pertain to the duration between the purchase and sale transactions, encompassing periods that can vary from several months and years down to mere seconds or minutes. Attaining profitability can also be accomplished through the practice of 'short selling', which involves the borrowing of cryptocurrency at a premium price, subsequently selling it, and repurchasing it at a depreciated value.

Gaining an understanding of the mechanics involved in cryptocurrency trading holds significant significance. It is feasible to attain immediate returns by closely monitoring market trends and assuming a more proactive approach in the management of your cryptocurrency investments. It necessitates a proactive daily examination of values and trends. This enables one to capitalize on higher and more immediate profitability, as opposed to enduring the fluctuations of long-term market cycles.

The advantages of acquiring knowledge in the field of cryptocurrency trading.

• You have the capability to capitalize on the brief periods of market volatility • You possess the capacity to leverage the temporary fluctuations in the market • You have the opportunity to exploit the momentary peaks and valleys in the market • You are equipped to benefit from the transient fluctuations in the market.

- You have the ability to exercise authority over the funds you have allocated to cryptocurrency.

- It is possible to attain greater frequency of short-term profits.

- Increased efficiency in the process of returning items • Quicker turnaround time for returns • Expedited returns process • Improved speed in the refund process • Enhanced timeliness of returns and refunds

The fundamental procedures for engaging in cryptocurrency trading

In order to engage in trading various currencies, it is essential to possess cryptocurrency wallets corresponding to the respective currencies.

In order to proceed, it will be necessary for you to become a member of a cryptocurrency exchange like Coinbase.

Begin by engaging in the trading of prominent cryptocurrencies such as Ethereum and Bitcoin.

Please contemplate the possibility of affiliating with an alternative currency exchange in order to engage in trading of coins that are not currently listed on Coinbase.

Maintain vigilant observance of emerging trends.

Please be aware that it is not necessary to purchase entire units of cryptocurrency.

Stay informed about the latest updates and developments regarding cryptocurrency by keeping track of blogs and news relating to the subject matter.

Maintain a comprehensive documentation of all financial transactions for the purpose of tax compliance.

Payment is required for transactions.

Please take into consideration that there is a significant variance among cryptocurrencies, and it is essential to note that substantial profits can be accompanied by substantial losses as well.

Chapter summary:

We have thoroughly examined the overarching framework pertaining to the practice of cryptocurrency trading. To summarize, let us now outline the key points that should be held in remembrance.

Participating in trading activities enables individuals to allocate their funds into cryptocurrencies temporarily, with the intention of capitalizing on fluctuations in market prices.

To engage in trading, it is necessary to possess a cryptocurrency wallet and participate in an exchange platform.

Engage actively in monitoring trends and deliberate upon the trading approach that aligns with your personal preferences.

Commence by engaging in the trading of well-established coins until you have gained sufficient confidence in navigating this particular market.

Please have a keen awareness of the tax consequences.

Your prompt initial action measure:

Allocate sufficient time to conduct comprehensive research on the subject of trading. Please conduct thorough research on the currencies, exchanges, and communities to make informed decisions. If you are eager to pursue trading as a serious endeavor, it is imperative that you allocate sufficient time each day to meticulously analyze your position. We encourage you to allocate a portion of your schedule at present with the intention of initiating this endeavor and evaluating its compatibility with your daily routine.

TRADITIONAL MONEY

Conception and pivotal stages (from the Gold Standard to the adoption of fiduciary currency)

Characterizing currency as an invention is a significant error. Currency is the culmination of an evolutionary process that has, at different periods, encompassed the diverse methods of exchange that have succeeded each other throughout history.

The fundamental premise of conducting commercial transactions involved adhering to the quintessential protocol of exchange and commerce, which specifically entailed the practice of barter.

The latter encompasses the trade of merchandise and the provision of services, contingent upon a condition of reciprocal advantage; however, this requirement is not the sole determinant.

The convergence and alignment of needs are crucial prerequisites for the actualization of the exchange.

In accordance with the aforementioned ancient means of transaction, two methods of payment were subsequently recognized by scholars as being pre-currency in nature.

The initial form of currency referred to as the "natural currency" involved the use of merchandise to facilitate the regulation of exchanges in situations of surplus. In contrast, the second illustration of pre-currency is exemplified by tool money. This mode of payment gained prominence during the 9th century B.C. and encompassed tools and everyday objects, which were utilized in barter transactions without compromising their inherent utility.

In conjunction with the pre-currencies, there exists a historically corroborated line of reasoning that posits debt as a fundamental element of early economies rather than barter.

In the region known as Mesopotamia, to be more precise, the ancient civilization of the Sumerians displayed their mastery of writing by inscribing the outstanding debts among different individuals on clay tablets, corresponding to specific quantities of goods.

This phenomenon gives rise to the issue of postponed exchanges, thereby establishing economic interaction on the foundation of social bonds and mutual confidence, which are extraneous to the barter system.

In due course, both prevalent types fell into obsolescence owing to the challenges associated with overseeing transactions involving substantial quantities. Consequently, the transition was made towards the utilization of metallic forms, which, when minted, served as a means to ensure and establish an inherent value, even when facilitated by private individuals.

The initial instances of the utilization of metallic currency were discovered in Lydia circa 500 B.C., and prior to that, in the Eastern region, particularly in China, around 1200 B.C.

In contrast to the Chinese predecessors, the Greeks, Persians, and subsequently the Romans opted for precious metals, thereby endowing currency with inherent value.

During the reign of Augustus in the Roman empire, the predominant medium of exchange was in the form of gold, accompanied by silver coins, which possessed their own recognized value for transactions.

In this particular system, the intrinsic worth of coins was undeniably tied to the substantial quantity of metal accessible for the purpose of minting.

Over time, this relationship gave rise to the occurrence of gradual inflation, which consequently impacted the depreciation of the coins' value.

This occurrence was addressed by implementing a reduction in the quantity of precious metal contained within the coins. From a historical standpoint, this practice represents one of the earliest instances of seigniorage employed by the imperial mints.

Throughout the course of centuries, the monetary system has experienced various transformations owing to circumstances such as the exploration of abundant silver reserves, resulting in a gradual shift towards the adoption of bimetallism.

The prevailing system in Europe remained intact until 1661, at which point the circulation of coins was superseded by the introduction of banknotes initiated by Sweden. It is worth noting that China is attributed with the earliest known utilization of banknotes in 800 AD; however, this practice was swiftly discontinued due to the detrimental impact of rampant inflation caused by excessive issuance.

These phenomena have been reproduced across Europe, wherein the minting of coins occurred without their worth being secured to a trustworthy commodity, such as gold.

Indeed, gold reserves constituted the foundation and criterion of issuance solely in the year 1816 in England, wherein the monetary unit was denoted by the gold pound, which was defined as precisely 113.0016 grams of untainted gold.

The legislation enacting the gold standard outlined three requisites:

The Royal Mint was obligated to purchase or sell unrestricted quantities of gold at a predetermined price;

There were no restrictions or constraints imposed on the import and export of gold.

The Bank of England was mandated to exchange bills and deposits for gold as necessary.

The quantity of gold possessed by the latter entity established the extent to which credit could be extended through the provision of deposits or banknotes, consequently impacting the banks' capacity to extend credit.

Hence, when analyzing the balance of payments, the inflows and outflows of gold in each nation resulted in alterations in the worth of monetary reserves, thereby directly influencing currency prices. Indeed, substantial influxes of gold would have resulted in an inflationary cycle, whereas significant withdrawals would have instigated a currency tumult.

The gold standard was the prevailing monetary system on a global scale during the period from 1870 to 1914, aiming to regulate and curb price inflation. This adoption of the gold standard was exemplified by the enactment of the Gold Standard Act in the United States in 1900. Among its significant implications was the establishment of the central bank through the Federal Reserve Act of 1913.

Within this monetary framework, the exchange rate system was firmly tied to the gold reserves, whereby each currency possessed a predetermined metallic parity, establishing an inherent mechanism for automatic adjustment. The outcome was a system of stable exchange rates among various national currencies.

The suspension of the Gold Standard occurred for multiple reasons during the First World War. Primarily, this is attributed to the influence the war wielded over trade and financial transactions. Furthermore, it is noteworthy that numerous nations faced the challenge of substantiating the alignment and adequacy of their gold reserves vis-à-vis the substantial issuance of banknotes to fund wartime expenditures. One more element that contributed to the crisis of the Gold Standard system, without a doubt, was the insufficiency of gold, thereby rendering it incapable of satisfying the requirements of diverse economic systems.

Due to these considerations, the decision was made to adopt a monetary regime known as the Gold Exchange Standard. In the nations where it was implemented, the domestic currency ceased to be exchangeable for gold but rather became exchangeable for foreign currency (specifically, the dollar) that could then be converted into gold.

This administration indeed facilitated the accumulation of foreign currency reserves, not limited to gold, with the objective of mitigating the strain on the latter.

Numerous economists, subsequent to the conclusion of the First World War and the onset of the Great Depression, identified multiple deficiencies within the Gold Standard framework. These shortcomings included the impracticability of nations augmenting their money supply to bolster economic recuperation, owing to the necessity of aligning gold reserves with the issuance of banknotes.

With the objective of addressing the issue of currency instability prevalent in that particular context, the international agreement known as the Bretton Woods agreement was ratified in 1944, thereby authorizing the adoption of the Gold Exchange Standard.

In the aforementioned system, fixed exchange rates were established among the currencies of different nations. Specifically, each currency's value was tied to the U.S. dollar, which alone had the convertibility to gold. The conversion ratio was set at a fixed rate of 35 dollars per ounce.

Through the Bretton Woods agreements, the dollar was indisputably established as the fulcrum upon which the equilibrium of the global economy hinged. This convention resulted in heightened pressure on the United

States' currency. Coupled with the expenditures stemming from the Vietnam conflict, it fostered a climate of mistrust towards the dollar. Consequently, numerous central banks opted to convert their reserves into gold.

The condition of the U.S. currency reached an unsustainable state until August 1971 when the then-president Richard Nixon issued a decree, rendering the dollar no longer exchangeable for gold, resulting in the termination of the fixed exchange rate system.

This crucial measure resulted in the implementation of fiat currencies, specifically payment instruments that are not supported by assets such as reserves of gold and consequently lack inherent value.

The trust individuals place in institutions assumes utmost importance within this context. It is worth noting that the government and the issuing central bank serve as the custodians of the value of fiat currencies, with their use being diligently regulated and lawfully guaranteed.

In this particular context, we refer to a fiduciary monetary system, as it is evident that individuals willingly accept fiat currency in return for commodities and services, relying on the belief that it will be universally acknowledged in future transactions.

An intriguing and essential element lies in the fact that trust serves as the defining factor that links the conventional monetary system to alternative currencies, which have emerged as a consequence of significant technological advancements, such as cryptocurrencies.

Blocks And Transactions

Now, let us proceed to discuss the subject of blocks and transactions. It is important for you to recognize that Bitcoin transactions do not adhere to the conventional remittance model. Instead, they bear resemblance to a communicative medium that imparts the stored value of Bitcoin from the sender to the intended recipient. It is imperative for us to highlight that there still exists a notable number of individuals who mistakenly perceive cryptocurrency as a tangible form of currency, akin to traditional coins, due to the visuals depicting the Bitcoin logo resembling a conventional coin.

Bitcoin and other cryptocurrencies serve as a symbolic embodiment of an individual's word, conveying their perceived worth. Once the communication is transmitted, it possesses a comparable value to currency or, to emphasize further, a valuable and precious resource such as gold. This embodies the fundamental nature of cryptocurrency.

Novice individuals frequently inquire, driven by curiosity, regarding the origin of funds within purported wallets in the absence of authentic currency.

Historically, it has been customary for us to carry currency and proceed to the marketplace located in the township's central square in order to engage in commerce. In the contemporary landscape, the town square has assumed an international character, serving as a digital hub and marketplace that can be effortlessly accessed through the internet. The value carriers function as tangible intermediaries within this virtual space.

As the originator, could you kindly elucidate the source of your coins? As the sender, you have three available methods to obtain coins within your designated address. One can obtain it through the act of mining, make a purchase, or receive remuneration from another individual in exchange for their product or service. The act of generating currency through mere imagination or fabricating numerical representations is impracticable as it violates the principles of authenticity and the impossibility of double spending.

The system effectively hinders the occurrence of these events solely due to its embedded code, which is integrated within the system.

Therefore, it is not possible to generate currency arbitrarily. The objective behind incorporating blocks into the blockchain network lies in the necessity of mining:

To enable miners to utilize a tangible asset in the physical realm, thereby facilitating the generation of a valuable asset in the virtual realm.

To bestow upon each coined unit or token an air of authenticity through the endorsement of previous utilization. As its usage increases, users become increasingly aware of the legitimacy and value it possesses. The blockchain technology eliminates the necessity for centralized governmental validation in order to confer legality and value.

It serves as a safeguard against counterfeiting, ensuring that only authorized users can undertake its verification and secure storage, thus eliminating the need for a centralized system governing the currency.

Fairness and Transaction

This forms the fundamental essence of the complete Bitcoin value transmission mechanism. For centuries, society has become accustomed to utilising paper currency due to its convenient storage and ease of use. Consider the scenario in which you are obliged to bear the burden of a satchel replete with gold while engaging in retail transactions. We are aware that our paper currency holds inherent value due to its legal declaration by the government. The production and distribution of goods are under the authority of the government.

Essentially, fiat currency such as the dollar bill or gold coin functions purely as a medium for the representation of value. The tangible benefit lies in the fact that this document holds the potential for sustenance acquisition or remuneration for one's labor. Currency functions as a means of exchange that facilitates streamlined and efficient transactions. Alternatively, in any other case, all of us would find ourselves compelled to visit the supermarket for the sole purpose of providing our services in exchange for a mere gallon of milk. Are you able to perceive the rationality behind this?

The value diverges from that of the carrier. When engaging in physical trades, we rely on conventional paper documentation; however, as we embrace electronic trading methods, the need for an electronic counterpart becomes imperative. It is widely acknowledged that printed currency originates from the governing authority, thereby instilling confidence in its recipients that the monetary value represented by the physical notes holds significant worth.

However, it is crucial to note that the worth of a currency is not contingent upon the trustworthiness of governmental institutions, rather it derives from the efforts and transactions of the individuals who utilize and exchange it.

In the realm of cryptocurrency, none of these conditions or factors are present—rather, the sole determinant of value for these digital currencies resides in the trust and confidence bestowed upon them by individuals, or more specifically, their users. How do users choose? They will analyze the historical performance of all the current cryptocurrencies. It is not solely Bitcoin, but also other cryptocurrencies such as Ethereum. It is imperative for them to possess credibility, as users will scrutinize their past track record. That serves as their initial premise.

The essence of human interaction lies within the exchange of value, which can solely be attained through diligent effort. Devoid of this essential element, the transition from physical trading to electronic trading would pose significant challenges.

Transactions

We acknowledge the fact that each transaction entails the transfer of a specific quantity of currency from an individual possessing it to another individual who is the intended recipient. In the event that your account does not possess any coin, you are unable to initiate any transfer. However, an individual holding a newly created address has the capacity to receive any quantity of coins. You have the ability to generate an unlimited number of addresses without encountering any restrictions. The quantity of addresses that can be generated aligns with each instance of private keys being created.

There are a total of 297 potential private keys that can be generated. Although the numerical value may seem modest when expressed in this manner, it assumes a considerable magnitude in written form.

One point five eight four five six three three times ten to the power of twenty-nine, or One hundred fifty-eight sextillion, four hundred fifty-six quintillion, three hundred thirty quadrillion.

Whose enumeration of such a quantity is conceivable?

The occurrence of a collision is highly improbable when considering statistical analysis. In other words, if you were to select a private key at random, the likelihood of obtaining a key that has not already been chosen is approaching negligible proportions.

The probabilities are altered when attempting to select a specific number, such as a personal date like a birthday or anniversary, and subsequently converting it into a hash. This hash is then utilized to generate both a public key and a Bitcoin address. It would not be unforeseen if the resulting number has already been claimed. The rate of collisions rises when a random number generator is not utilized to select a private key on one's behalf.

After selecting a random number, it can be documented and subsequently processed through a SHA256 converter in order to obtain the corresponding hash. Subsequently, you can utilize it as your private key and attempt to derive the corresponding public key, thus enabling the creation of a Bitcoin address.

In the event that you possess a Bitcoin application on your computer system, it will autonomously create an account and generate both the public and private keys multiple times at your discretion.

When initiating a transaction, party A is transmitting a communication to party B, denoting the transfer of XBTC. It is not solely directed towards B but rather encompasses every individual on the network. Once A has transmitted the message, all nodes within the network are in a state of attentive reception. Remember gossip protocol? The system will initiate its pointing process and add the message to the queue, triggering the nodes to commence the verification process to determine if your message is permissible. In the event that all processes are successfully executed and the transaction undergoes thorough verification and confirmation, it is envisioned that B, the designated recipient, shall assume the legitimate ownership of the coin.

The coin's essence is bestowed with animate characteristics through the transaction, leading to the transaction's inherent value owing to the coin. There are two stipulations that merit consideration. First and foremost is the unavailability of a coin that can be obtained without cost. Starting from the initial transaction, every coin acquires an inherent worth, derived from the computational effort invested by miners during the block creation process.

The subsequent aspect pertains to the portion of the coin's value that is allocated based on the net demand it generates. An increase in net demand signifies the intrinsic value will experience a trade premium. An adverse demand implies that the coins will lose their encoded intrinsic worth, ultimately rendering them valueless.

In the realm of commerce, the worth of a particular entity can inherently remain isolated; however, in order to effectively convey this worth, it must be articulated in relation to another commodity or object of significance. Within the realm of cryptocurrency, there exists a resilient exchange market that possesses the capacity to precisely ascertain the worth of nearly any other esteemed fiat currency. For instance, when considering the value of BTC in terms of US dollars, it has experienced a notable escalation, starting from a negligible amount of pennies to BTC, subsequently reaching $5, then advancing to $50, and further surging to $500, until ultimately soaring to a peak of $20,000.

That constitutes a substantial sum, and traditional economists continue to grapple with comprehending the appearance of such figures.

The value of BTC in the physical realm has been determined by the existence of fiat currency. Certain individuals argue that this could render BTC impractical as a prominent form of currency in the forthcoming years. Nevertheless, Bitcoin was not intended to supplant national currency, in any case.

Key considerations regarding transactions:

Transactions are communication entities dispatched across an entire network and disseminated by nodes through the utilization of the gossip protocol.

All transactions are irreversible. Once you have transmitted the items, it is not possible to retrieve them.

An irrevocable transaction ID is allocated to each transaction.

Each transaction identification number contains a record of the sender's and recipient's addresses.

After introducing the transaction ID, we will now proceed to further examine it.

Transaction ID

The transaction ID is allotted into a pool after the validation of its legitimacy by the network nodes. Upon entering the pool, the transaction IDs along with the header information (including the date and timestamp, nonce, and block number) are consolidated within the block and initiate the hashing process.

After undergoing the process of hashing, the block will yield a distinct combination of alphanumeric characters. Modifying even a single character within the entirety of the text will result in a transformation of the series from lowercase to uppercase, thereby causing the hash to differ. Alterations are not feasible as they would merely cause disruption to the entirety of the process. In the event of an unauthorized hacking attempt aimed at reversing a transaction within the system, the hash discrepancy and non-functioning nonce would render such an endeavor futile, ultimately resulting in the failure of the respective block.

Each block includes the hash of the preceding block, alongside additional components, in the event that you intend to modify a transaction that is six blocks deep. When the block is subjected to hashing, the resultant hash will undergo a modification, consequently affecting the subsequent hash in the sequence.

If your intention is to persist in modifying a specific block, it will necessitate a significant magnitude of computational resources to modify even a solitary transaction. Furthermore, after two to three subsequent blocks, the returns garnered from such endeavors become inconsequential in comparison to the exertion invested.

The system necessitates exerting authority over the outcome of a specific hash, as it enables miners to engage with the puzzle that iterates through hashes until the desired format is achieved. The initial miner will be entitled to the reward. After the block is ultimately hashed, it will be appended to a sequence and the subsequent block processing will commence, incorporating the block hash of the preceding block.

Block

The file size of each transaction is approximately 100 kilobytes, however, the actual value may differ, although it should not surpass 1 megabyte. As various transactions are amassed, the nodes proceed to enqueue them for the miner to adopt and subsequently incorporate them into blocks.

Therefore, a collective set of transactions is denoted as a block. These transactions are collected. As an example, let us consider the block number 520763. This information will be visible upon conducting a search for blocks based on their numbers within the system.

The miners shall generate a block. When the miners retrieve the blocks, it is customary for them to take them in their original state. Nevertheless, miners retain the freedom to select the transactions they wish to include or exclude. The miners shall be granted incentives should they opt for the blocks exhibiting the most significant financial contributions. A prescribed fee is applicable for Bitcoin transactions, yet senders retain the flexibility to augment the amount in order to hasten the confirmation duration. Consequently, using this quantity as a basis, miners will proceed to prioritize the transactions and subsequently incorporate them into a block. Subsequently, they will commence the process of puzzle-solving, referred to as mining, to produce the block.

After the mining process concludes, the blocks will be allocated a specific block number and organized in a consecutive order. Each block will be allocated a distinct composition and transaction ID of its own. There shall be no instances of replication. Subsequently, every block will be meticulously linked to the preceding block, while the subsequent block will be meticulously linked to the current block.

It is imperative to highlight that transaction IDs possess uniqueness for every individual transaction. No two IDs are identical, and the number cannot be reused. It will be impossible to make changes in the transaction using the same ID.

Blocks confer upon individual transactions the assurance of usability and the validity of existence.

Miscellaneous Matters And Concerns

Revised GHOST Implementation

The protocol commonly known as the "Greediest Heaviest Observed Subtree" (GHOST) was initially pioneered by Yonatan Sompolinsky and Aviv Zohar in December of 2013. The rationale behind GHOST is that blockchains with fast confirmation times currently experience a diminished level of security due to a high stale rate. This is because blocks require a certain amount of time to disseminate throughout the network. If miner A mines a block and then miner B happens to mine another block before miner A's block disseminates to B, miner B's block will ultimately be rendered ineffective and will not enhance network security. Additionally, there is a concern regarding centralization. For instance, if miner A represents a mining pool with a hashing power of 30% while miner B has a hashing power of 10%, miner A will encounter a 70% risk of generating a stale block. This is because 30% of the time miner A produced the last block and therefore receives mining data immediately. On the other hand, miner B will face a 90% risk of producing a stale block. Therefore, assuming that the duration of the block interval is sufficiently brief in order to yield a high rate of stale transactions, A will exhibit significantly greater efficiency primarily due to its larger size. By merging these two outcomes, it is highly probable that blockchains that generate blocks at a rapid pace will result in one mining pool attaining a significant percentage of the network's hashpower, effectively establishing control over the mining process.

According to the studies conducted by Sompolinsky and Zohar, GHOST addresses the initial concern of network security compromise by incorporating stale blocks into the determination of the "longest" chain. This means that not only the parent and further ancestors of a block are considered, but also the stale children of the block's ancestors (referred to as "uncles" in Ethereum terminology) are taken into account when determining which block has the highest cumulative proof of work supporting it. To address the second issue related to bias caused by centralization, we propose an expansion of the aforementioned protocol by Sompolinsky and Zohar. In addition, we introduce a mechanism where stale blocks can be registered on the main chain to receive a block reward. Specifically, a stale block would be entitled to 93.75% of its base reward, while the nephew block that includes the stale block would receive the remaining 6.25%. Transaction fees, nonetheless, are not allocated to uncles.

Ethereum utilizes a streamlined iteration of GHOST that solely descends to a depth of five levels. More precisely, a stale block can solely be deemed as an uncle by its parent's 2nd to 5th generational offspring, excluding any block with a more distant kinship (e.g. Individual who is the descendant of a parent from the sixth generation, or the offspring of a grandparent from the third generation. This action was undertaken due to various factors. Initially, the incorporation of infinite GHOST would introduce numerous complexities into the determination of which uncles are valid for a given block. Additionally, the utilization of unlimited GHOST in conjunction with appropriate compensation within the Ethereum network eradicates the motivation for miners to engage in mining activities on the primary blockchain rather than on the chain of a public attacker. In conclusion, the calculations indicate that the five-level GHOST algorithm, coupled with incentivization, achieves a level of efficiency exceeding 95% even when operating with a block time of 15 seconds. Additionally, miners possessing 25% of the total hashing power exhibit marginal gains of less than 3% in terms of centralization.

Fees

Due to the fact that each transaction recorded in the blockchain necessitates the network to undergo the process of downloading and verifying it, a regulatory mechanism, commonly involving transaction fees, becomes necessary to counteract any potential misuse. The conventional approach, employed in Bitcoin, is to have entirely discretionary charges, depending on miners to function as the guardians and establish fluctuating thresholds. This particular approach has garnered significant approval within the Bitcoin community, primarily due to its "market-based" nature. This framework enables the interaction of supply and demand forces between miners and transaction senders to determine the pricing. However, the issue with this line of reasoning lies in the fact that transaction processing cannot be equated to a market. While it may seem logical to perceive transaction processing as a service provided by the miner to the sender, the reality is that every transaction included by a miner must be processed by every node in the network. As a result, the overwhelming majority of the cost associated with transaction processing is actually borne by third parties, rather than the miner who makes the decision of whether or not to include it. Therefore, it is highly probable that tragedy-of-the-commons issues will arise.

Nonetheless, it appears that this imperfection within the market-driven system, when presented with a specific erroneous simplifying assumption, remarkably nullifies its own effects. The argument can be stated as follows. Suppose that:

1. A transaction results in k operations, providing the reward of kR to any miner who includes it, wherein R is determined by the sender and both k and R are approximately discernible to the miner prior to inclusion.

2. Every node incurs a processing cost of C for each operation. All nodes possess equal efficiency.

3. There exist a total of N mining nodes, each possessing precisely equivalent

processing power, namely. one divided by N of the total

4. No non-mining full nodes are present.

A miner would be inclined to execute a transaction provided that the anticipated benefit surpasses the associated expenses. Hence, the anticipated remuneration can be expressed as kR/N, considering the miner's probability of processing the next block is 1/N, and the miner incurs a straightforward processing cost of kC. Consequently, miners will incorporate transactions in which the ratio of kR/N to kC is greater than 1, or when the quantity R exceeds NC. Please take note that R represents the transaction fee paid by the sender and serves as a minimum estimate of the sender's benefit derived from the transaction. Additionally, NC refers to the total cost incurred by the entire network when processing an operation. Therefore, miners are motivated to include only those transactions in which the overall societal benefit outweighs the associated costs.

Notwithstanding, various significant deviations from these underlying assumptions exist in reality:

1. The miner incurs a greater expense in processing the transaction compared to the other verifying nodes, as the additional verification time delays block propagation, thereby increasing the probability of the block becoming obsolete.

2. There do indeed exist full nodes that are not engaged in the process of mining.

3. The distribution of mining power may ultimately result in a significant disparity of wealth and influence in practical terms.

4. Regulators, individuals with political agendas, and individuals with harmful intentions who wish to disrupt the

network do indeed exist, and they possess the ability to strategically establish contracts that incur lower costs compared to the costs paid by other validating nodes.

Based on the first enumerated point, there exists a proclivity for the miner to incorporate a reduced number of transactions. Furthermore, the second point contributes to an escalation in NC. As a result, these two effects do overlap to a certain extent, mitigating their combined impact. The principal concerns pertain to points 3 and 4. To address these issues, we propose the implementation of a dynamic cap, wherein no block shall exceed BLK_LIMIT_FACTOR times the value of the long-term exponential moving average in terms of operations. To be precise: the value of blk.oplimit will be calculated as the integer division of the product of blk.parent.oplimit,

EMAFACTOR minus one, blk.parent.opcount multiplied by BLK_LIMIT_FACTOR, and the inverse of EMA_FACTOR.

BLK_LIMIT_FACTOR and EMA_FACTOR are currently designated as constants with values of 65536 and 1.5, respectively. However, it is anticipated that these values will be subject to modification following additional analysis.

Number 6
CHAINLINK

Number 6: Chainlink

Introduced in June 2017 by the esteemed fintech enterprise from San Francisco, Chainlink serves as a Smart Contract. Developed to foster secure interoperability between smart contracts across multiple blockchains,

Chainlink acts as a reliable blockchain middleware. Its primary objective is to facilitate the integration of key off-chain resources, such as data feeds, web APIs, and traditional checking account payments, into the realm of smart contracts.

The developers hold the belief that smart contracts, despite their potential to revolutionize various industries through the substitution of conventional legal agreements, face limitations in their ability to effectively interface with external systems due to the underlying consensus protocols associated with blockchain technology.

The LINK token and LINK Network are the designated names for the native token within the Chainlink ecosystem. The developers intend to augment the application and usability of smart contracts on a global scale by means of API and other platforms.

What are Smart Contracts?

Smart contracts represent computer programs that are deployed and executed within decentralized infrastructures, such as a blockchain. Whereas a conventional contract delineates the conditions that govern a legally enforceable relationship, smart contracts utilize cryptographic code to enforce said contractual association.

Once specific conditions are met, smart contracts are triggered and their execution ensues. Moreover, the presence of these smart contracts on a decentralized network ensures that their code remains unaltered and their execution remains uninterrupted by any party. Through the prevention of modifications, smart contracts establish a binding agreement between all parties involved, thereby engendering a form of relationship that is not reliant on trust in any individual party.

Source: Chainlink

As per the assessments made by the developers of Chainlink, limitations can be observed in the current framework of smart contracts implemented on the blockchain. As an illustration, due to the inherent support for smart contracts on a blockchain and the consensus mechanism achieved by miners in relation to transaction data based on the blockchain, smart contracts are incapable of interfacing with external resources such as data feeds, API, or conventional banking systems.

The conventional approach to solving this problem involves employing a blockchain middleware known as an "oracle."

What are Oracles?

Oracles play a crucial role as blockchains inherently lack the capacity to directly retrieve data from external sources. Oracles serve as intermediaries responsible for locating and validating real-world events, which are subsequently transmitted to a blockchain for integration into smart contracts. It offers the external data required to activate the execution of smart contracts upon the fulfillment of predetermined conditions, such as the receipt of a payment or a price fluctuation.

Oracles are external entities that operate with a centralized control, lying outside the purview of the blockchain's consensus mechanism. Consequently, the issue at hand pertains to the reliability of data obtained from an oracle in the context of smart contracts. Due to the ability of smart contracts to autonomously execute functions based on predefined conditions, it is imperative that oracles furnish information that is both accurate and reliable.

Certain oracles subscribe to notarization as a means to authenticate their data, whereas others espouse the manual input of unstructured data by human agents. Nevertheless, according to the developers of Chainlink, such oracles exhibit certain imperfections. The former is flawed due to the potential recursive need for verification, while the latter may entail significant costs, resource demands, and an inability to furnish real-time information.

As per the developers' statements, the Chainlink network facilitates the seamless integration of data feeds and other APIs directly into smart contracts in return for Chainlink tokens. Individuals of this category are commonly known as Node Operators. They enable data providers, as well as other entities like payment providers or service providers, to directly offer their API-based services to a smart contract in exchange for LINK tokens. The developers propose that this decentralized infrastructure facilitates the integration of data, off-chain payments, and APIs in a coherent manner that is both scalable, secure, and auditable.

The Chainlink Network

The Chainlink Network comprises a decentralized infrastructure of Chainlink Nodes that facilitate the sale of specific data feeds, APIs, and diverse off-chain payment functionalities directly to smart contracts.

The Chainlink Network consists of two distinct components, namely the on-chain and off-chain elements, which must collaborate in order to facilitate the provision of the service. The network was constructed with a capacity for upgradability, thus permitting the replacement of its various components as more advanced techniques and technologies emerge. The on-chain segment of the network employs oracles that are capable of filtering the requested metrics by a party to a smart contract, in accordance with a services level agreement (SLA).

By utilizing this data, Chainlink obtains the responses of the oracles to the Service Level Agreement (SLA) queries. These responses are then organized and analyzed using reputational and aggregation models. Subsequently, Chainlink presents the ultimate consolidated outcome of the query, which can be incorporated into the smart contract.

Chainlink Token

To address the requirements outside the Chainlink system, the establishment of the LINK token is essential as it serves as the designated currency for facilitating payments to Node Operators. As per the statements of the developers, the utilization of the LINK token is necessary to carry out this particular operation. The tokens' demand and value are closely linked to the quantity of operators providing off-chain services to the system.

As the utilization of the Chainlink platform increases, the intrinsic value of LINK tokens is expected to appreciate due to their role as a digital currency within the platform. Certain commentators have put forth the notion that the inclusion of the LINK token within the project may be superfluous, as alternative cryptocurrencies are equally capable of furnishing remuneration to operators. Furthermore, the presence of these alternative cryptocurrencies would inherently incentivize oracles to remain within their network and ensure a continuous access to their own data.

The reputation system, an integral component of the Chainlink network, intends to incentivize node providers with a substantial volume of secured LINK tokens by bestowing them with sizable contracts. In the event that they fail to provide precise information, they will face penalties in the form of deducted tokens. This appears to be a highly advantageous system for token holders, as the act of securing a larger number of tokens in contracts leads to a reduction in supply, subsequently resulting in an increase in token prices.

Price Predictions

According to the analysis provided by tradingbeasts, it is estimated that the price of LINK could potentially hover at approximately $24.081 by the conclusion of 2021. Furthermore, it is projected that by the culmination of 2024, the price may surge to around $33.223.

It is assessed that Chainlink represents a highly favorable investment opportunity, with projections indicating sustained price growth over an extended period of time. Digitalcoin envisions a scenario where the price of Chainlink (LINK) reaches $32.48 by the conclusion of 2021.

WalletInvestor's algorithmic prediction indicates a strong bullish sentiment regarding the potential future value of Chainlink. It is believed that the LINK price has the potential to appreciate to $56.834 within a span of one year. According to their analysis of the prevailing market conditions, it is projected that the rate will increase to $226.161 by the conclusion of 2026.

According to the projections provided by Longforecasts, it is anticipated that the price of Link could fluctuate within the range of $25.39 to $31.51 by the conclusion of 2021. Furthermore, it is predicted that by mid-2025, the price may experience an upward surge and surpass the value of $51.00.

The Inherent Shortcomings Of Decentralised Finance

The decentralisation argument stands as one of the most significant points in favor of cryptocurrencies, as observed in many discussions. Decentralised finance pertains to the notion of substituting conventional financial entities like brokerages, exchanges, and banks with a blockchain-based resolution, enabling individuals to transact directly with one another. The underlying concept is to eliminate intermediaries, which results in increased investment returns for individuals and reduced borrowing costs. Another factor contributing to the decision to eliminate banks is the prevailing sense of profound mistrust towards the banking system among a significant portion of the population, which persists in the aftermath of the 2008 financial crisis.

The primary issue with the concept of decentralised finance lies in the fundamental requirement for the adoption and endorsement of the associated currency by a central bank or government in order for it to function effectively. As previously demonstrated, unless the currency attains universal adoption, including the capability to fulfill tax payment obligations, it remains devoid of any practical value. Another significant concern pertains to the lenders' capacity to obtain collateral for the purpose of securing loans. By utilizing a decentralized system underpinned by cryptocurrency, individuals have the opportunity to borrow cryptocurrency while providing cryptocurrency as collateral. That's like going to the bank and asking for a mortgage for $100,000 but giving them $120,000 as collateral. The primary objective of the loan is to provide you with the opportunity to secure funds against the asset you intend to acquire. Should the lender not possess a legitimate entitlement to said collateral, the entire contract becomes devoid of value.

The notion of availing oneself of the option to borrow or lend funds while obtaining more advantageous interest rates through the elimination of intermediaries appears commendable. However, it is imperative to deliberate upon the practical implications entailed by such a proposition. Frequently, concepts that appear commendable in theory fail to yield positive results when implemented in practical settings.

Consider the instance of a home mortgage for the purpose of purchasing a residence. In accordance with customary practice, the customer would typically visit the bank to initiate the loan application process, during which the bank shall evaluate the customer's credit history and ascertain the feasibility of the loan amount requested. They also assess the appraisal value of the property being acquired to ensure that, in the event of loan default by the borrower, the property can be liquidated to recoup the funds. As a component of the lawful transfer of the property, the bank will possess a proprietary right to the property in the event that the loan is not timely reimbursed in accordance with the terms stipulated in the loan agreement. These inspections are subject to governmental and financial regulatory oversight, having evolved over the course of a century to establish a mutually beneficial risk equilibrium for both financial institutions and their clientele. The existence of these financial regulations is essential to promote the protection of both parties involved in the transaction and to uphold the efficient operation of our contemporary economies.

Now, let us contemplate the identical scenario within a decentralized financial framework. The primary concern in this matter pertains to the incorporation of the digital currency. Should it lack the endorsement of the government or central bank, it is highly unlikely that any sensible individual would deem it as a suitable means of payment for a considerably valuable asset such as a house. There is no individual who meets this criterion, therefore it is prudent for us to proceed with the assumption that payment will be made using a fiat currency.

Upon seeking a loan for the property, the customer is required to provide cryptocurrency assets exceeding the loan's value as collateral. At present, the decentralized lending institutions necessitated collateral that valued twice the amount of the fiat currency loan. Let us overlook the evident issue with that proposition and instead consider the scenario where the customer possesses the necessary collateral and consequently obtains the loan, dispensed in the form of fiat currency. After receiving the funds, the customer proceeds to transfer the money to the property owner, who subsequently completes the transfer of ownership of the property to the customer.

In the context of a decentralized financial system predicated on cryptocurrencies, the loan collateral shall not encompass physical assets, but rather denote a specific quantity of cryptocurrency. The possibility of the lender establishing a proprietary interest in tangible assets in the event of the borrower's nonpayment is eliminated within a decentralized framework. So, what are the consequences in the event that the loan is not repaid? The lender receives the pledged collateral as security for the loan.

The issue at hand is readily apparent; it represents an unfavorable arrangement for the customer. The primary concern pertains to their obligation to possess collateral valued at twice the amount of the loan in order to secure said loan. Consider a prospective homeowner who is aiming to purchase a property valued at £100,000 as a first-time buyer. In a system characterized by decentralization, an amount of £200,000 in cryptocurrency assets would be required to secure the loan. This blatantly undermines the intended objectives of the loan and, in a genuine economic context, will prove futile for an overwhelming majority of individuals. When availing a bank loan, a mere 5% deposit or a sum of £5,000 suffices, as the bank employs the property as collateral. Mortgage lending constitutes a fundamental pillar of contemporary economies, contingent upon the lender's acquisition of property as collateral.

Furthermore, it should be noted that the interest rates are significantly unfavorable, contrary to the assertions made by proponents of cryptocurrency. As of the present moment, a widely utilized decentralized cryptocurrency lending platform provided loans commencing at an Annual Percentage Rate (APR) of 4.5%. By contrast, concurrently, financial institutions are providing loans with a minimum annual percentage rate of 1.44%.

The paradox of a decentralised financial system based on cryptocurrency lies in the fact that it remains dependent on a fiat currency for its functioning, thereby diminishing its claim to true decentralisation. It is undeniable that centralized banking systems are not as negative or malevolent as some might portray them to be. A centralized banking system is the enabling factor that grants individuals the ability to purchase their residences or vehicles. It enables the receipt of a currency exhibiting a stable value, thereby facilitating the acquisition of essential goods and services required for sustenance, such as nourishment, housing, utilities, and protection. Centralised financial systems put man on the moon, they allow your job to exist, they allow roads to get built, they allow hospitals, schools, emergency services and government all to exist.

Contemporary centralized financial systems are the fundamental pillars that enable our society to uphold its current existence.

Considering the inclusion of risk, unfavorable interest rates, excessive collateral prerequisites, volatility, and absence of regulation synonymous with a decentralized financial system, it becomes difficult to fathom how individuals residing in developed nations would genuinely embrace it. Contrary to prevailing perceptions, our existing financial systems effectively fulfill their purpose, and while occurrences such as the 2008 financial crisis emerged as a consequence of this system, regulations have continuously evolved to mitigate the likelihood and severity of such events.

Optimizing The Well-Being Of The Body And Mind

A frequently disregarded aspect of achieving success in investment involves maintaining good health. Although it may not be readily apparent, upon deeper contemplation, it becomes evident that maintaining equilibrium in all areas of one's life holds significant significance. In broad terms, it is crucial to uphold a harmonious relationship between one's mental and physical well-being. This is the factor that enhances your concentration and optimizes the utilization of your energy.

When experiencing high levels of stress, fatigue, and negativity, it becomes challenging to gather one's focus to the extent necessary for optimal productivity in trading endeavors. For example, in the event that one is engaged in a research endeavor, it is conceivable that adequate concentration on the graphical representations and numerical data essential for monitoring may become unattainable. This can potentially lead to the implementation of trades in a disorganized manner. It goes without saying that this will not produce optimal outcomes.

In addition to customary suggestions such as maintaining a nutritious diet, engaging in regular physical activity, and managing stress levels, it is pertinent to acknowledge that tending to one's psychological welfare forms an integral aspect of a prosperous trading strategy. Overall, investing can become quite burdensome. Although the possibility of experiencing hair loss due to trading

FOREX is not inherent, the intensity of the activity can occasionally be substantial. For instance, in situations where one experiences considerable strain due to a series of consecutive setbacks, there is a possibility that one may feel compelled to engage in trading activities that entail a greater degree of risk. Furthermore, you might experience a profound sense of pressure to compensate for your financial setbacks. While it is unpreferable for individuals to experience defeat, it is crucial to handle losses with composure to the best of your ability. Defeats and setbacks are an intrinsic aspect of the human experience and should thus be regarded accordingly.

An additional prevalent concern among investors, particularly day traders, pertains to their tendency to overly fixate on conducting extensive research. If one becomes entangled in the demands of trading, there is a risk of developing an excessive fixation on engaging in research and executing trades. Consequently, you may find yourself dedicating excessive hours to your workstation. This may result in the formation of unhealthy behavior patterns, such as prolonged periods of sitting. Furthermore, it can have a detrimental impact on one's mental well-being, given that trading entails a significant cognitive process.

Hence, accomplished investors perceive FOREX as merely another undertaking within their daily routine. They establish predetermined routines and endeavor to adhere to them to the greatest extent feasible. They endeavor to establish a timetable that they deem suitable. They also conclude their time at the terminal as a means of mitigating excessive screen exposure. By engaging in this activity, individuals can rejuvenate their cognitive abilities and return with heightened concentration.

Specifically, in instances where an excessive quantity of data and information becomes burdensome, allocating time for respite can facilitate the cognitive processing of the assimilated information. This elucidates the reason why participating in sports, or partaking in any form of physical exertion, can aid in mental clarity. By engaging in this action, you can regain your momentum and enhance your concentration and vitality. It is highly undesirable to find oneself in a situation where one is engaging in laborious efforts. If anything, the practice of engaging in FOREX trading is an activity that should bring you pleasure. Therefore, coercing oneself to engage in such actions will invariably hinder the attainment of favorable outcomes. Please consider allowing time for rest. Ensure the proper management of your emotional and psychological well-being. You will discover that this approach greatly simplifies matters.

Rsi Trading Strategy

The Relative Strength Index (RSI) is a momentum indicator that provides insight into the level of asset or cryptocurrency buying or selling activity. In essence, the Relative Strength Index (RSI) is an oscillating tool that computes a range between two contrasting values, thereby gauging the magnitude of price fluctuations and the velocity at which they occur.

Given the unpredictable nature of stock and crypto markets, the utilization of technical indicators provides assistance in plotting optimal entry and exit strategies. Hence, RSI serves as a dependable indicator for cryptocurrency traders.

Certain traders employ the Stochastic RSI methodology as a means to elevate their understanding of market sensitivity. This particular technical indicator is a synthesis of the stochastic oscillator formula and the RSI, displaying a numerical range from 0 to 100. Would you desire to learn the most favorable aspect? Continue reading to acquire further knowledge.

What is RSI?

J. The RSI was initially introduced by Welles Wilder Jr. in 1978. In the customary fashion, the Relative Strength Index (RSI) identifies fluctuations in the value of cryptocurrency or stock assets within a standard timeframe of 14 intervals. Nevertheless, the timeframe can be extended or shortened based on the trader's investment horizon. It is quantifiable in units of weeks, days, hours, or even minutes.

The equation for Relative Strength Index (RSI) can be expressed as follows:

The formula for RSI can be stated as follows: RSI equals 100 minus the quotient of 100 divided by the sum of 1 and RS.

RS can be calculated by dividing the average profit by the average loss.

The average profit is calculated by dividing the sum of profits over a given time frame (e.g., 14 periods) by the number of periods.

The average loss is obtained by dividing the sum of losses incurred within a given time frame by the duration of the said time frame.

Trading platforms provide users with the ability to access the Relative Strength Index (RSI) and perform automatic calculations of its values. Hence, there is no requirement for calculation. After the application of the tool to your trade, the RSI line graph will be rendered beneath your market chart.

RSI is frequently employed for the purpose of ascertaining prevailing market trends. The fundamental approach to utilizing an index involves purchasing an asset or cryptocurrency when it demonstrates an increase in value, and subsequently divesting from it when it exhibits further growth.

In general, the purchase of an asset tends to be higher when the relative strength index (RSI) value exceeds 70%, whereas sales typically increase when the RSI value drops below 30%.

The purchase of an asset in surplus serves as a definite indication of an emerging pattern of deterioration. Conversely, a security that is excessively sold is indicative of an ascending trend. The current scenario depicts a depletion of strength in the asset's performance, accompanied by a gradual accumulation of momentum.

RSI serves as an originating point for a variety of trending trading methodologies. An additional frequently employed trading strategy involves the purchase or sale of assets when the relative strength index (RSI) reaches or surpasses the midpoint level. This marks the inauguration of a novel trend.

A bullish trend can be observed when the relative strength index (RSI) exceeds 50. When the temperature falls below 50 degrees, it signifies the initiation of a negative trajectory.

Traders frequently employ a midline cross-trading strategy, wherein they consider the 70/30, 50/50, or 60/40 ratio as levels of resistance and support for discerning bullish or bearish trends.

When the level of resistance is impacted, it may lead to a reversal of the prevailing trend. Hence, traders are advised to respond accordingly.

What is RSI Divergence?

Apart from its fundamental purpose, the divergence of relative strength index provides a superior indicator for the market. Engaging in transactions based on divergence enables enhanced confidence and minimizes the likelihood of misinterpreting signals.

An RSI divergence denotes a discrepancy between the oscillator and the present price action. This illustrates both bearish and bullish stances.

The swiftly expanding disparity indicator indicates the subdued market price movement depicted on the chart, as well as the irregular fluctuations in the RSI's highs and lows. This indicates that the cryptocurrency is experiencing an upward trend. However, inexplicably, this phenomenon has yet to be accurately portrayed in the fluctuations of market prices.

Conversely, a bearish divergence transpires when the chart exhibits both high and low levels while the RSI indicates a high value. This serves as an indication of an imminent retracement in prices.

What does RSI indicate?

The fundamental pattern of an asset guarantees that the indicators are interpreted accurately. The Relative Strength Index denotes the level at which the cryptocurrency transitions from a bullish trajectory to the onset of a bearish trend. Constance Connie Brown, a market analyst, advocates for an innovative concept instead of adhering to the conventional wisdom that the optimal distribution for profitable assets is 70/30.

According to his statement, the signal with the highest sales figures registers at approximately 30%, while the signal with the greatest level of purchase activity stands at around 70%. Hence, it is possible that the Relative Strength Index (RSI) may approach a value of 50% during the downward trend, as opposed to the conventional threshold of 70%. In order to more effectively ascertain extremes, the majority of traders employ horizontal trend lines.

Nevertheless, one effective approach to circumvent inaccurate RSI signals entails utilizing trading indicators that correspond to the prevailing trend. For instance, employing bearish signals for an asset in a bearish trend and bullish signals for an asset in a bullish trend can help prevent false RSI indications. Signal usage.

A concise handbook on RSI translation

A bullish trading signal is generated when the Relative Strength Index (RSI) crosses above the threshold of 30. Should the value drop below 70, it indicates a downward trend.

When a cryptocurrency's RSI surpasses 70, it indicates an excessive level of buying activity and is likely poised for a turning point. A Relative Strength Index (RSI) value below 30 indicates an oversold indication.

In an ascending trajectory, the Relative Strength Index consistently remains above the threshold of 30 and frequently achieves a level of 70. In juxtaposition to declining patterns, the RSI indicators exhibit a propensity to descend below 30 but refrain from surpassing the threshold of 70. This concise manual aids in the identification of the positive attributes of a trend and the observation of an impending shift in direction.

As an illustration, should the RSI indicator neglect to reach the 70 mark amid different price fluctuations in an upward trend, it inevitably drops below 30, indicating a feeble trend that is susceptible to decline.

The contrasting trend diverges significantly at the opposite end of the spectrum. If it does not descend below 30 or ascend beyond 70, the trend can be deemed as feeble. Consequently, it has the capability to undergo a complete inversion.

Time Period

The default time frame for RSI is set at 14 periods. This is due to the fact that numerous traders, particularly those engaging in swing trading, deem this time frame to be suitable. However, it is commonly observed that the majority of day traders deem it advisable to adapt their strategies in order to accommodate a more responsive oscillator.

Day traders with a preference for short-term trades tend to favor a time frame spanning from 9 to 11 in the morning.

Typically, individuals engaged in long-term trading often establish a time threshold ranging between 20 and 30.

It is contingent upon the degree of sensitivity exhibited in each particular instance.

The cryptocurrency market has shown a refusal to accept RSI swing patterns.

The RSI indicator offers a prospect to cultivate diverse trading strategies. The technique of swing rejection relies on the correlation between the RSI's reaction to signals indicating an increase or decrease in buying activity. Similar to variations, swing rejection is categorized into expeditious and bearish.

The classification of blushing swing rejection encompasses four distinct patterns of movement:

The occurrence of RSI initiates a bearish indication.

It dates back more than three decades.

It descends into another trough without encountering the threshold of oversold conditions.

RSI surpasses its present peak.

This methodology is comparable to the incorporation of a horizontal trend line onto the graphical representation of prices. The chart below clearly illustrates the graphic depiction of the repudiation of abrupt fluctuations. Following an increase in sales, the Relative Strength Index (RSI) exhibits a 30% upward movement and showcases a decreased rate of rejection. It triggers the signal once it is elevated.

Bearish swing rejection bears a resemblance to blush swing rejection. In addition, it comprises four primary divisions:

The relative strength index (RSI) has entered into the overbought region.

It is less than 70%.

It reaches another zenith without regressing into the realm of excessive purchases.

The Relative Strength Index (RSI) ultimately breaches its prevailing trough.

Similar to other trading strategies, this signal proves to be dependable when it aligns with comparable prevailing long-term trends.

The Contemporary Realm Of Blockchain

Exploring Blockchain Mining and Investment Opportunities

Blockchain Mining

Within the contents of this discourse, we shall employ the bitcoin as an illustrative example within the realm of digital currencies. As you explore the topic of bitcoin mining, it is essential to bear in mind the overarching subject at hand, which pertains to the blockchain and its associated mining activities. In essence, mining in this particular context pertains to the incorporation of novel block records (transactions) into the openly accessible ledger of blocks. It is important to recall that these blocks constitute a sequence of transactions or blocks within the digital ledger commonly referred to as the blockchain. Once these records are recorded, the blockchain makes it public to other connected networks or nodes of the completed block. The node linked to the blockchain utilizes this data to distinguish between lawful and unlawful bitcoin transactions, as well as identify instances where coins are being spent again after they have already been used. Due to the utilization of the "proof-of-work" mechanism in bitcoin, it is imperative for every transaction or block to include this hashcash "proof-of-work" in order to attain legitimacy and acceptance. Upon the arrival of a new block on the blockchain, every node connected to the blockchain undertakes the task of verifying the "proof-of-work" associated with the block. Subsequently, once this verification process is successfully concluded, the block or transaction is duly validated. This process can be completed within a matter of seconds. After undergoing validation, the new block is subsequently appended. Thus, the daily increment of blocks is effectively regulated and maintained at a consistent level. It requires significant resources and was deliberately crafted for this specific intent. It enables every blockchain-linked node to maintain transaction security and achieve a consensus that is resistant to tampering.

However, mining also serves the purpose of introducing newly minted digital currency into the system. When newly minted coins come into existence, miners are granted compensation in the form of transaction fees. These newly minted coins are disbursed through a decentralized mechanism, instilling trust in the overall system's security. Cryptocurrency miners contribute to the maintenance of network security through their consensus-based validation of transactions. Mining plays a crucial role in maintaining equitable conditions, as well as guaranteeing the safety, security, and stability of the network.

What is the operational mechanism behind the mining process? Allow us to briefly examine the process of how hard currency or paper money is circulated, for illustrative purposes. The government makes determinations and subsequently grants authorization in regard to the timing of currency production and the manner in which it is disseminated. In this regard, however, the bitcoin does not require the endorsement of a central government for its production and dissemination. It represents a digitalized, decentralized form of currency, operating independent of any centralized governmental authority. Miners employ specialized software applications and intricately engineered mining hardware to generate or extract these currencies. They employ software applications to address computational operations and, as a result, receive a predetermined amount of virtual currencies. It represents an intelligent approach to acquiring the currencies and likewise serves as an inspirational example for individuals aspiring to engage in the mining of these digital currencies.

Blockchain Mining Hardware

Cryptocurrency mining hardware is specifically engineered to produce "proof-of-work." There exists a wide selection of hardware options available, but your selection will depend on various factors such as the desired coin type, hashing algorithm, and the overall satisfaction levels reported by users. Could you kindly elaborate on the aforementioned hashing algorithm or hashrate? The rate governs the frequency at which a miner engages in attempts to solve a cryptocurrency block within a given time frame. The higher the number of attempts to solve a cryptocurrency block, the increased likelihood of successfully solving the block and the enhanced efficiency of the mining hardware. The metric used to quantify the rate at which hashes are computed is expressed as hash per second (H/s). We may consider utilizing units of Kilohash (KH/s), Megahash (MH/s), Gigahash (GH/s), Tetrahash (TH/s), and Petahash (PH/s). Presented in the subsequent table are comprehensive particulars regarding the hardware pertaining to the foremost three cryptocurrencies.

You are presented with a diverse array of hardware options to select from. If one were to consider mining, the aforementioned options are highly recommended.

Blockchain Mining Software

The primary responsibility for the development of a digital currency lies with the mining hardware, however, the mining software also plays an essential role. The linking of the mining hardware to the blockchain network is necessary. Similar to the consideration process involved in selecting hardware, several factors need to be taken into account when determining which software program will effectively support your cryptocurrency mining endeavors. These considerations encompass the operating system and the specific form of cryptocurrency you intend to develop. As stated in the previous chapter, a plethora of distinct digital currencies were in circulation by 2017, totaling over nine hundred. Each of these currencies possesses its own dedicated software. Hence, it is important to note that if one intends to develop a currency like Litecoin, for instance, the software employed in the creation of Dogecoin may not be compatible or suitable for the intended purpose. It is necessary to acknowledge, however, that certain software has the capability to generate multiple varieties of cryptocurrency. Presented below are a selection of software applications from which you may make a choice.

Example:

The ZOTAC 750 T 1GB is capable of achieving a hashrate of 5.35 MH/s when mining Lyra 2v2.

The XFX 7990 exhibits a hashrate of 21.8 MH/s when mining the x11 algorithm.

The XFX 7990 is capable of producing a hashrate of 28 MH/s for Quark.

The XFX R9 290x black edition demonstrates a hash rate of 32 MH/s for Ethash.

Mining Difficulty

Put succinctly, this entails the assessment of the arduousness pertaining to the quest of discovering a fresh block or the strenuousness involved in unearthing a hash that falls beneath a designated benchmark. The metric is regularly modified in accordance with the level of computational power employed by participating miners. The existence of a global block difficulty necessitates that valid blocks must attain a hash value below this predefined threshold. The level of difficulty is modified after the completion of every 2,016 blocks, in accordance with the duration it took to discover the preceding 2,016 blocks. If the discovery rate of one block per ten minutes persists, it would require a time span of two weeks to identify a total of 2,016 blocks. If the previous 2,016 blocks took longer than two weeks to find, the difficulty is reduced. On the contrary, if the duration of 2 weeks or less was sufficient to discover 2,016 blocks, it is then duly anticipated that the level of difficulty has been amplified.

Blockchain Investment

Given the abundant availability of this information, one might naturally ponder the means by which they can partake in the investment opportunities that arise within this continuously expanding economy of the blockchain. It would be advisable to inquire about the appropriate measures to prevent financial loss, such as "What steps should I take to safeguard my funds?" What information do I need to be aware of? When would be the optimal timing for investment, and what strategies can be employed to maximize potential returns?

It is highly recommended that you consider investing in blockchain due to its unparalleled growth potential, which distinguishes it as the most rapidly expanding investment opportunity currently accessible. The number of individuals utilizing the network is consistently increasing on a daily basis at an exponential rate, subsequently resulting in the favorable expansion of the investment. Let us consider Facebook. Presently, it possesses a valuation surpassing $30 billion. It is progressively expanding on a daily basis. Over six billion individuals are presently utilizing it, and every discerning business proprietor aspires to allocate resources into it. Why? There are solely three steps that need to be undertaken: investment, patience, and financial gain. This assertion holds true for blockchain technology as well. Consider these statistics:

In the year 2010, the number of users was approximately 10,000. In the year 2012, there was a surge in the numerical value, reaching a count of 100,000. In 2014, two years subsequent to this, the user count witnessed a surge, reaching a significant milestone of 1,000,000. Moreover, in the preceding year, an unprecedented figure of 10,000,000 users was registered. With this rate, in 2020, it is estimated that about 100,000,000 users will be actively using blockchain technology. With the expansion of the network user base, there will be a corresponding increase in investment. Undoubtedly, it is now opportune to consider the prospect of investing your funds and anticipating the accrual of substantial profits in due course. It currently stands as the most promising investment opportunity, with certain individuals hailing it as unparalleled since the advent of the Internet. Smart move!

Blockchain technology has the potential to eradicate financial deceit through a variety of means. Banks can go bankrupt. Funds have the potential to be depleted even when securely stored within a financial institution, and in the event of an insufficient capital base, the subsequent response would be an apologetic acknowledgement. Blockchain technology, nonetheless, serves as a mathematical assurance for the preservation of economic autonomy.

Prior to considering investment, it is crucial to dedicate sufficient time to acquiring at least a rudimentary understanding of computer functionality and operation. Should you choose not to do so and have the intention to invest in blockchain technology, it is highly probable that you will incur financial losses, potentially jeopardizing the funds you have diligently earned.

It should be noted that for every account, a password is essential. Devise a password that you can readily recall, or alternatively, record it in writing to facilitate prompt retrieval in the event of forgetting. Additionally, ensure that the password you select is not easily discernable by others. It is essential to ensure that your funds do not fall into inappropriate or unauthorized possession.

Acquire the knowledge and skills to create data backups. If you have harbored an aversion towards the use of antivirus programs, endeavor to develop an appreciation for their utility and diligently maintain their updates. This measure will provide security for both your computer and your accounts.

Prior to considering investment in the cryptocurrency market, it is strongly advisable to enhance your proficiency in computer literacy.

The subsequent course of action entails having a deliberate discussion to ascertain the precise proportion of your earnings that you intend to allocate for investment purposes. Recognize the presence of potential risks, particularly as an inexperienced investor, and as a precautionary measure, endeavor to commence your investment endeavors with a capital allocation ranging from 1% to 10% of your overall income. This holds significant importance, given the remote possibility of immediate fulfillment of expectations, provided you possess adequate proficiency in computer skills. As you gain proficiency with the system, gradually augment your stake or investment.

It is important to emphasize that the blockchain investment opportunity should be considered as a long-term investment with aspects of trust. It generates returns and gains over a period of time. If you happen to be an individual seeking immediate financial gains, this may not align with your objectives. Establish a reasonable investment timeframe spanning between three to eight years, considering the nascent stage of blockchain technology.

Conduct thorough market research, carefully analyze the prevailing trends, accurately assess the market fluctuations, and strategically determine the opportune moments to engage in buying or selling activities.

Valuable Insights provided by Professionals for Miners and Users in the Field of Cryptocurrency

Achieving success on the blockchain network demands meticulous analysis and calculation. However, profound gratitude is extended towards individuals who have attained triumph in cryptocurrency trading, for their invaluable insights and recommendations. It can be perceived as devising an itinerary for a remote destination that remains unfamiliar to you. While you may initially be uncertain about what to anticipate, receiving direct insights from individuals who have already experienced the destination can greatly enhance your knowledge and assurance in making the decision to venture there. By offering firsthand accounts encompassing aspects such as the locale, culture, and living conditions, their input serves to fortify your confidence in embarking on this journey. What initially appears to be a perilous undertaking will swiftly transform into a captivating and delectable escapade. In this article, we will examine the factors that have contributed to certain individuals achieving significant success with cryptocurrency. Additionally, we will provide detailed instructions on how to effectively utilize the recommendations included within the provided content.

Privacy Tips

An essential aspect for all individuals utilizing blockchain technology is the ability to navigate the digital realm and engage in transactions while ensuring a substantial level of confidentiality and anonymity. Each day, individuals engage in transactions involving digital currencies with a combined value of millions of dollars. We are aware that our personal commercial transactions are not of public concern, thus necessitating our heightened requirement for privacy. Given that the blockchain, which serves as a digital ledger, is typically accessible by all interconnected nodes, it consequently results in widespread awareness of fund transfers among individuals. This situation can potentially endanger our online interactions with the public and render us vulnerable to a range of malicious entities whose objective is to monitor users and their online behaviors. Cybercriminals also present a peril, and how can we effectively discern between cybercriminals and legitimate business collaborators when face-to-face encounters are not feasible? It is imperative that we take measures to safeguard our well-being. Outlined underneath are three measures that can be undertaken to enhance the level of online security.

Establish a connection with a proxy.

Browse on TOR

Obtain a Virtual Privacy Network (VPN).

Every security approach entails its own set of benefits and drawbacks, associated expenses and constraints, as well as inherent strengths and vulnerabilities. Below, you will find a concise analysis of three available alternatives pertaining to online security. Following this, you will possess the capacity to make an astute determination regarding the means by which you may enhance your online privacy.

Proxy Security

We have been aware of proxies for an extended period of time. What is a proxy? It is a device that is strategically deployed at a specific location for the purpose of allowing Internet users to redirect their network traffic through it prior to accessing the broader Internet. Proxies represent the primary technological advancement of the Internet when it comes to establishing remote connections. However, how might they safeguard your online commercial transactions? They offer security and privacy by functioning similar to a firewall, effectively thwarting unauthorized intrusion, thus providing significant protective measures. However, certain routers outperform standard proxies in terms of security. Several proxies are available at no cost, however, from an Internet security perspective, gratuitous proxies may not always be advisable. Gratis does not guarantee security or dependability at all times. The concept of being unrestricted in the realm of online privacy may entail reduced data transmission capacity and vulnerability in terms of security. They have the ability to adopt an alternate IP address for certain processes, yet their capacity to elude more sophisticated forms of surveillance falls short. If you happen to be an individual with constrained financial resources, proxy security is a suitable option to consider. However, it is important to bear in mind that such security measures have inherent limitations.

Browse on TOR

TOR is an acronym that stands for The Onion Router. By deploying numerous relays, this method effectively conceals your connection from thorough surveillance. Each of these connections renders it exceedingly challenging to track the origin of every action back to the IP address responsible for generating said actions. It can be likened to a collective of intermediaries operating in unison. The TOR browser can be downloaded at no cost and it is available in both iOS and Android versions. Certain government entities with exceptional proficiency in information technology, such as the CIA and the NSA, retain the capability to monitor individuals even when they employ a TOR browser, as they possess the means to detect its usage. Despite its cost being zero, it performs admirably.

Network infrastructure that enables secure and private remote connectivity, known as Virtual Private Network (VPN).

Among the three security alternatives, the Virtual Private Network (VPN) stands out as the most optimal solution for augmenting your online privacy during any given circumstance. This is due to the fact that Virtual Private Networks (VPNs) employ encryption, resulting in encrypted online activity for users who utilize encrypted commands. The Virtual Private Network effectively manages all online traffic without any limitation to a particular program or web browser. The range of functions available on the TOR browser is constrained, but when using a virtual private network (VPN), your entire online connection becomes safeguarded. Consequently, you need not be concerned about whether certain activities are permissible or not. However, it is of high quality, therefore requiring a monetary investment, yet one aspect remains certain. It provides the most optimal safeguarding measures on the internet. When selecting the optimal VPN, several criteria merit consideration:

• Expense and velocity

• The efficacy of their customer service • The efficiency of their customer service • The level of effectiveness demonstrated in their customer service • The quality and effectiveness of their customer service • The degree to which their customer service proves effective

Do they maintain records of their activities?

• Which devices are compatible? • Which devices are eligible for support? • Which devices are approved for use?

The geographical placement of the VPN host is an additional aspect to take into account, as it holds significance due to the general preference for maintaining anonymity while browsing the internet. Governments may require certain VPN hosts to provide logs of their tracking activities, based on the geographical location of said hosts. Considering that you are financing such services, a certain standard of treatment can rightfully be anticipated, and it is only fair that you receive the finest quality care. Select a VPN provider that ensures a strong and effective customer support experience. The identification of good customer service lies in the range of contact options provided by the VPN host. Ideally, an exemplary customer service should provide telephone, email, and chat as essential modes of communication. If the prospective host fails to offer anything more substantial, it would be advisable to reconsider your decision. Certain VPN services are compatible with the iOS operating system, whereas others are compatible with Android devices. One additional aspect to take into account is whether the VPN provider permits multiple connections. Through the utilization of a solitary subscription, one should possess the ability to establish connectivity across diverse devices. It would be deemed less acceptable if you were required to incur a subscription fee for each individual device you utilize.

Other Useful Tips

Utilize all available resources to your advantage. Certain individuals do not fully appreciate the utility of the diverse Internet search engines. What is the potential downside? Ensure that you allocate time to thoroughly acquaint yourself with the fundamentals of blockchain trading through periodic inquiries, making use of search engines to address any queries you may have. You will undoubtedly be astonished by the extent of knowledge you will acquire. With assuredness and effortless ability, you will engage in trading activities alongside seasoned professionals in the industry, readily offering assistance to those in need.

Please record your wallet recovery phrase, wallet identification number, and password. Prior to initiating the transfer of funds to your wallet, ensure that you secure them in a location where the risk of misplacement or loss is minimal. The wallet recovery phase facilitates the process of creating a backup for your data. Alternative suggestion: "While various recommendations may abound on safeguarding one's online endeavors from external threats, the wallet recovery stage serves as a self-imposed shield against one's own potential mishaps." Upon the establishment of your wallet, it is always advisable to create a backup for your wallet. It is imperative that you do not overlook or disregard this section, as it holds substantial importance in determining your level of achievement. There are two categories of keys that are linked to your wallet: a public key and a private key. This stage of wallet recovery will ascertain the preservation of these keys within your file. Provided that the keys are safeguarded, the blockchain network possesses the capability to effortlessly retrieve your balance at any given point in time. Users have the flexibility to store the keys in various external storage mediums, including but not limited to portable drives, external hard drives, flash drives, optical disks, mobile phones, or even in written form on a physical piece of paper. Additionally, it is possible to store it on a cloud-based backup system, such as the icloud on iOS devices or Dropbox on Android and Windows devices. However, it should be noted that the reliability of the cloud storage system is not absolute. It is advised to encrypt the data prior to uploading it onto any cloud-based storage platform.

It is advisable to thoroughly verify the accuracy of your transaction details prior to confirming and sending by clicking the "Enter" button. It is a frequently observed occurrence for individuals to verify a bank statement prior to presenting it to the cashier, despite the remediable nature of any detected errors. If we are able to exert such diligent measures in scrutinizing banking records, it becomes even more imperative to thoroughly verify online transactions within blockchain networks prior to their execution. The reason is simple. Once the "Send" button has been pressed, it becomes irretrievable. It is crucial to verify the quantity of digital currency intended for transfer, ensuring that the accurate amount is being sent. Additionally, please ensure to verify the cryptocurrency address you plan to send to. It is imperative that you avoid any errors.

Keep separate wallets. Individuals have the freedom to generate and retain multiple digital wallets, as there exist no restrictions on the quantity of wallets one may create. If all of your digital currency assets are concentrated within a solitary wallet, the prospect of facing various forms of online exploitation becomes a distinct possibility. Certain individuals with expertise and professional backgrounds maintain distinct digital wallets to serve various purposes. They possess distinct wallets designated for the purpose of remitting and transferring funds, a separate wallet meant specifically for accepting payments, and an additional wallet exclusively dedicated to their savings. You may choose to embrace this approach, which is likely to yield successful outcomes in your case as well.

It would be beneficial for you to diversify your savings beyond a web wallet. Possessing and managing a web wallet undoubtedly offers convenience; however, it is recommended that it be managed akin to a checking account, wherein we store funds intended for immediate use. Acquire the necessary skills to manage your online wallet with identical efficiency. There have been security breaches reported in certain web wallets. In the interest of maintaining your security, it is advisable to only retain a restricted sum of money within your online wallet. In the event that your wallet becomes subject to unauthorized access, the extent of any potential loss will be minimized. It is crucial to bear in mind that in the event of a financial loss on the blockchain network, the funds become irretrievable. Despite your potential efforts to involve law enforcement and initiate an investigation, the probability of successfully recovering your funds remains considerably minimal.

Make every effort to enhance your digital privacy. Do refrain from developing the practice of disclosing your passwords or keys to any individual. Your wallet address or public key functions as an equivalent to your bank account number, while your private key serves as a counterpart to the PIN associated with your account, verifying transactions associated with that particular account number. Exercise caution and refrain from disclosing your financial information to unauthorized individuals or malicious entities. It is imperative to always maintain the confidentiality of this information. It is always advisable to maintain a respectful distance from unfamiliar individuals. Given that blockchain technology operates on a transparent network accessible to all interconnected nodes, it becomes effortless to place trust in unknown business counterparts. Should you become excessively acquainted, however, it is likely that they will commence an inquiry into the valuation of your assets. One potential course of action is to endeavor to obscure the connections between your distinct wallets, such as the spending wallet and the saving wallet, by executing fund transfers between them via a mixing service or specialized programs designed to safeguard your privacy and anonymity.

Despite the storage of your digital currency holdings in a device such as a computer-based wallet, it does not guarantee complete immunity from malicious attacks. Various types of viruses and malware have the potential to infiltrate computer systems, such as the notorious Trojan horse. Hence, it is imperative to acquire a reputable antivirus software. Additionally, it is advisable to securely store the private key of your wallet in an offline medium as an additional safeguard against potential attacks. It may be stored on a flash drive or USB key. Furthermore, it is advisable to employ encryption on your private key to render it futile if it were to be acquired by unauthorized individuals. Without decryption using the requisite password, the key would be rendered inaccessible and therefore unusable. In the event that you opt to encrypt your private key, it is crucial to remember your password, as this could result in even yourself being denied access to your digital wallet.

www.ingramcontent.com/pod-product-compliance
Lightning Source LLC
Chambersburg PA
CBHW050241120526
44590CB00016B/2174